{ Introduction }

The quotations that follow are taken from Jyotish and Devi's weekly blog, *A Touch of Light*.

The paintings are by Nayaswami Jyotish.

The poem at the end, later adapted by Paramhansa Yogananda into a well-known chant, was written some hundred years ago by one of India's great spiritual emissaries.

If you would enjoy reading any of the blogs themselves, please refer to the listing of sources on the concluding page.

{ *Day 1* }

The secret of living fearlessly is **meditation.**

Now I am entering the inner Temple of God communion. Let this time be sacred.

Devi, "Tourist or Pilgrim" | *Half Dome*

Jyotish

The secret of living fearlessly is **never to compare.**

Gyanamata, Yogananda's most advanced woman disciple, was once faced with a severe test.

When she prayed to God, she felt it was not His will that she be spared that experience.

Immediately she knew the prayer God would receive:

"Change no circumstance of my life. Change me."

Jyotish, "The Secret Is Never to Compare" | *Divine Friendship*

Day 3

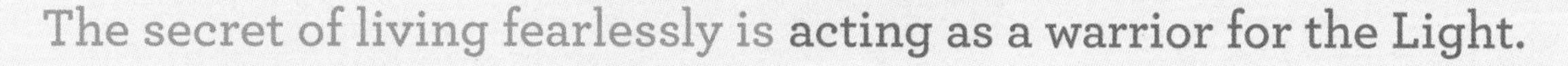

The secret of living fearlessly is acting as a warrior for the Light.

God's light is within me and around me.

With the sword of faith in my hand,
with the love of God in my heart,

I am a warrior of light.

I join my brothers and sisters everywhere
to overcome fear with faith,
hatred with love,
and disease with health.

We all are warriors of light.
We fill the world with God's light.

Jyotish and Devi, The Warrior of Light affirmation | *Master & the Spiritual Eye*

Jyotish

{ *Day 4* }

The secret of living fearlessly is surrendering to the Divine Will.

God opens doors for us **every day...**

Jyotish, "Say Yes to Life" | *Spirit & Nature*

{ Day 5 }

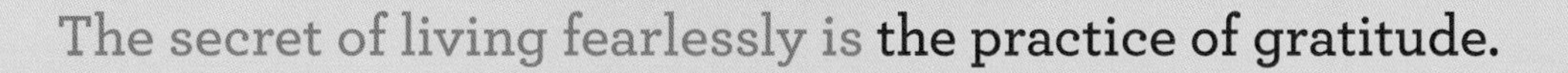
The secret of living fearlessly is **the practice of gratitude.**

I am grateful for my life,
exactly as it is.
I am thankful for this day.
I welcome every hour.
Thank you, God.
Thank you, God.

Jyotish, "Saved by the Guru" | *Divine Splendor*

The secret of living fearlessly is remembering your true potential.

Remember always your true potential: a radiant being **united with God.**

Devi, "Does Satan Exist?" | *Devi's Source*

Jyotish

{ Day 7 }

The secret of living fearlessly is asking, "Who's in charge here?"

God speaks when we converse in His language: utter, selfless love.

Devi, "When God Speaks" | *Devotion*

{ Day 8 }

The secret of living fearlessly is a balanced life.

When you realize that activity and meditation are really one, you will be able to find a still center at the heart of even the most trying circumstances.

Jyotish, *How to Meditate: A Step-by-Step Guide to the Art and Science of Meditation* | Master & Mt. Hood

{ Day 9 }

The secret of living fearlessly is acceptance of what is.

Don't resist or run away from change, or pray that circumstances be different. Instead, try to embrace the only change that is lasting: personal transformation.

Devi, "The Best Way to Deal with Change" | *The One in All*

Jyotish

{ Day 10 }

The secret of living fearlessly is offering kindness to others.

If kindness is a cure, then **we heal our own consciousness** when we give back love. When you are hurt by others, try to reverse the energy, for only light can dispel darkness; only love can heal hate.

Jyotish, "Unifying Principles" | *River of Light*

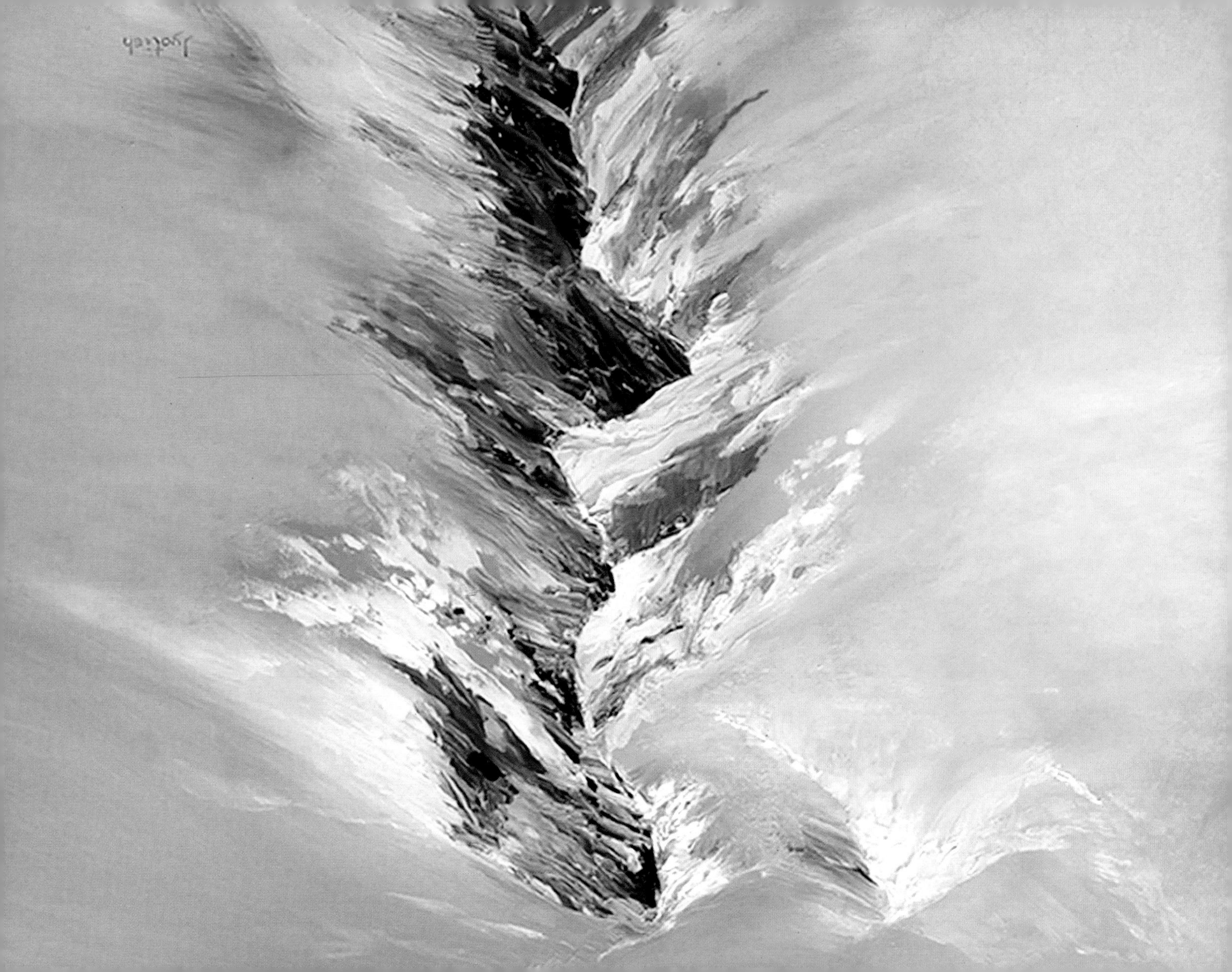

{ *Day 11* }

The secret of living fearlessly is stillness.

The process of transformation requires inner discipline to focus the mind on whatever we're doing, and perseverance until we begin to change from the inside.

We might call this process the "Art of Becoming."

In the heart of stillness
lies the key to lasting meaning and joy.

Devi, "The Art of Becoming" | *Mist & Dawn*

{ Day 12 }

The secret of living fearlessly is focus.

It starts with **intention**, is built by effort, gradually forms into a habit, and finally becomes a way of life.

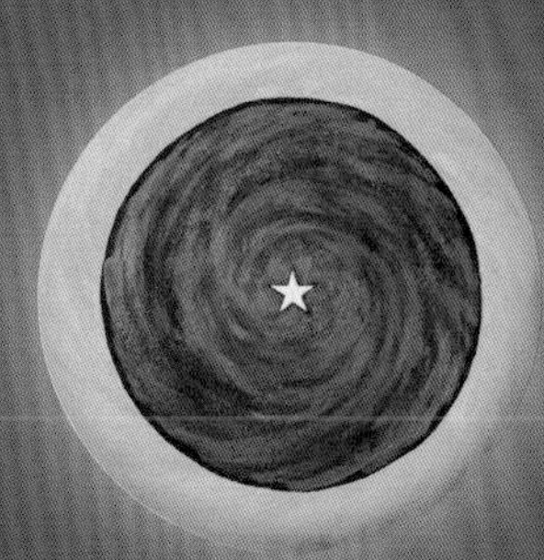

Jyotish, "Focus" | *Meditation on the Spiritual Eye*

The secret of living fearlessly is cultivating compassion.

Tear down those walls around your heart, and let God's forgiveness, compassion, and love shine into it.

Devi, "Does Satan Exist?" | *Opalescent Falls*

Jyotish

{ Day 14 }

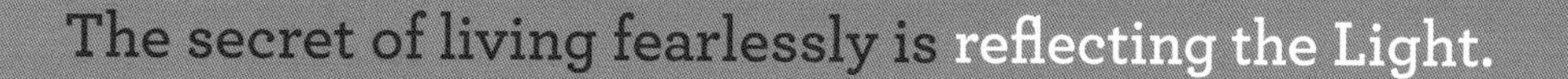

The secret of living fearlessly is reflecting the Light.

The moon generates no light of its own; it only reflects the light of the sun. Similarly, the ego is but a dim reflection of the soul, God's spark within each of us.

Jyotish, "The Eclipse" | *Moonlight Meditation*

Jyotish

{ Day 15 }

The secret of living fearlessly is **self-discipline.**

Counter little desires with will power and self-discipline.

Devi, "How to Control Desires" | *Northwest Coast*

Jyotish

{ *Day 16* }

The secret of living fearlessly is genuinely forgiving others.

The ultimate gift of forgiveness is this: It helps us to rise above the dualities of passing joy and sorrow and experience the true joy of unity within everything.

Devi, "What Forgiveness Gives Us" | *Divine Tenderness*

{ *Day 17* }

The secret of living fearlessly is staying solution-oriented.

Let the Divine solve the problem for you.

Three-pronged approach to finding solutions:

1. Clarify your feelings.
2. Visualize the outcome.
3. Let the steps become apparent.

Jyotish, "Solutions" | *I Am Always with You*

{ Day 18 }

The secret of living fearlessly is feeling your unity with all.

Judge no one, but accept all as expressions of God—as part of your own Self.

Devi, "Searching for Gold" | *We Are Thine*

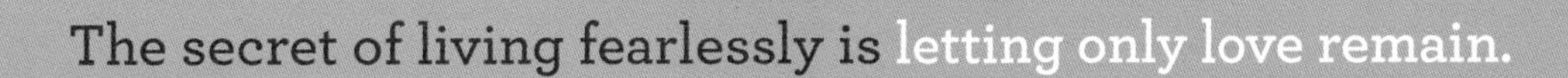

If my name, possessions, occupation, and very identity are all stripped away, let only love remain.

Jyotish, "Till Only Love Remains" | *Master with the Children*

{ Day 20 }

The secret of living fearlessly is lifting up your gaze.

Look upward and affirm, "I awake in Thy light! I am joyful! I am free! I awake in Thy light!"

Devi, "Lift Up Your Eyes!" | *Meditation on the Moonrise*

{ *Day 21* }

The secret of living fearlessly is **sharing.**

Sharing is vital for everyone wanting success and happiness, because it unleashes one of the most powerful forces in the universe: the Law of Abundance. That which you give to others will increase; that which you withhold will diminish.

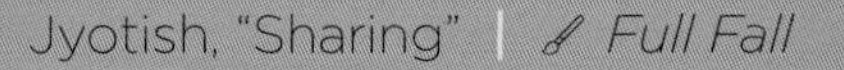

Jyotish, "Sharing" | *Full Fall*

{ Day 22 }

The secret of living fearlessly is embracing your fears.

Whatever fear you are now facing, try to see the divine Presence behind it. God is coming to you as that particular problem to help you **overcome your fears.** Accept it willingly, even joyfully if you can.

Devi, "Embrace Your Fears" | *Pomo Eagle*

Jyotish

{ Day 23 }

The secret of living fearlessly is cooperating with grace.

When we love God, He will play with us, but always by giving us His blessings.

Jyotish, "When We Cooperate with Grace" | *Amazing Grace*

The secret of living fearlessly is training yourself to see opportunities.

When we look at the challenges we face in our life or in the world at large, it's easy to feel discouraged, or perhaps even hopeless.

The secret to navigating rough water, however, is to be aware of the rocks in your path, but look for where the currents are flowing freely.

Where others see only obstacles, train yourself to see opportunities.

Devi, "Seeing the Possibilities" | *To the Mountaintop*

Jyotish

The secret of living fearlessly is finding calmness in the midst of activity.

Time is like a river on which you are floating. You can never occupy more than one place at any moment. Just focus your whole attention on where you are right now, and let the river take care of itself.

Jyotish, "Finding Calmness in the Midst of Activity" | *Wavecrest*

{ *Day 26* }

The secret of living fearlessly is **controlling the reactive force.**

When beset by the winds of karmic storms, think: "I will use a power **greater than my own** to overcome this test."

Devi, "Weathering the Storm" | *Vastness*

{ *Day 27* }

The secret of living fearlessly is releasing old hurts.

Refusing to release old hurts and disappointments only produces pain and suffering for yourself and others.

Negative thoughts and memories can be neutralized in a step-by-step manner:

1. Accept what happened.
2. Forgive everyone involved.
3. Express gratitude.
4. Feel love: real, heartfelt love.

Jyotish, "Overcoming Conflict" | *Divine Aspiration*

Jyotish

The secret of living fearlessly is dissolving the ego.

Swami Kriyananda once said, "The whole purpose of the spiritual path is to dissolve the ego. It is done by longer, deeper meditation, and seeing God as the Doer in everything."

Jyotish, "Dissolving the Ego" | *Infinity*

The secret of living fearlessly is discovering the joy within you.

Paramhansa Yogananda gave us these words of encouragement: “If you have made up your mind to **find joy within yourself,** sooner or later you shall find it. Seek it now, daily, by steady, deeper and deeper meditation within.”

Devi, “Trusting First Impressions” | *The Light of Mellow Joy*

The secret of living fearlessly is doing what you can.

When the goal is difficult or subtle and beyond your control, don't give up. Do what you can, and don't worry about the rest. A journey of a thousand miles is made up of millions of small steps. Take the steps that are within your capacity, always stretching yourself a little so that you don't get complacent.

Jyotish, "Do What You Can" | *I, the Cosmic Sea*

Jyotish

{ *Day 31* }

The secret of living fearlessly is
standing unshaken amidst the crash of breaking worlds!

**Claim the power within you
Error to defy!
The world may change
or disappear,
But truth can never die!**

Swami Kriyananda, "Go On Alone!" | *Waves of Bliss*

Marching Light*

A poem by

Swami Rama Tirtha

1

No, no one can atone me.
  Say, who could have injured,
And who could atone me?
  No, no one can atone me.

2

The world turns aside
  To make room for me;
I come, Blazing Light!
  And the shadows must flee.

3

I come, O you Ocean!
  Divide up and part;
Or parched up and scorched up,
  Be dried up, depart.

4

O Mountains, beware!
  Come not in my way;
Your ribs will be shattered
  And tattered today.

5

O Kings and Commanders!
  My fanciful toys!
Here's a Deluge of fire,
  Line clear! My boys!

6

Advisers and Counsellors!
  Pray, waste not your breath.
Yes, take up my orders,
  Devour up, ye, Death.

7

Go, howl on, O winds,
  O my dogs! howl free.
Beat, beat, Storms!
  O my Bugles! blow free.

8

I ride on the Tempests,
  Astride on the Gale,
My gun is the Lightning,
  My shots never fail.

9

I chase as an huntsman,
  I eat as I seize
The hearts of the mountains,
  The lands and the seas.

10

I hitch to my chariot
  The Fates and the Gods.
With Thunder of cannon
  Proclaim it abroad:

11

Shake! shake off Delusion,
  Wake! wake up! Be free,
Liberty! Liberty!
  Liberty! OM!

*Swami Rama Tirtha, *In Woods of God-Realization* (Delhi, I. M. H. Press, 1915) 474–75.

{ Sources }

The underlined references below are internet links which, when typed into one's browser, will call up the blog in question. The blogs have also been collected in a series of three books available from the publishers—*Touch of Light*, *Touch of Joy*, and the new (forthcoming in 2021) *Touch of Peace*—in which the blogs are listed in order by their date of publication.

Day 1: "Tourist or Pilgrim": joyiswith.in/20. *Touch of Light* 11/14/13
Day 2: "The Secret Is Never to Compare": joyiswith.in/21. *Touch of Light* 11/21/13
Day 3: "The Warrior of Light affirmation." Instruction on how to practice affirmation: joyiswithin/51
Day 4: "Say Yes to Life": joyiswith.in/23. *Touch of Joy* 4/9/15
Day 5: "Saved by the Guru": joyiswith.in/24. *Touch of Love* 1/26/17
Day 6: "Does Satan Exist?": joyiswith.in/25. *Touch of Love* 8/17/17
Day 7: "When God Speaks": joyiswith.in/26. *Touch of Joy* 9/17/15
Day 8: *How to Meditate: A Step-by-Step Guide to the Art and Science of Meditation*. joyiswith.in/27
Day 9: "The Best Way to Deal with Change": joyiswith.in/28. *Touch of Love* 6/8/17
Day 10: "Unifying Principles": joyiswith.in/29. *Touch of Love* 6/29/17
Day 11: "The Art of Becoming": joyiswith.in/30. *Touch of Love* 7/20/17
Day 12: "Focus": joyiswith.in/31. *Touch of Love* 7/27/17
Day 13: "Does Satan Exist?" joyiswith.in/32. *Touch of Love* 8/17/17
Day 14: "The Eclipse": joyiswith.in/33. *Touch of Love* 8/24/17
Day 15: "How to Control Desires": joyiswith.in/34. *Touch of Love* 8/31/17
Day 16: "What Forgiveness Gives Us": joyiswith.in/35. *Touch of Peace* 3/14/19
Day 17: "Solutions": joyiswith.in/36. *Touch of Peace* 1/24/19
Day 18: "Searching for Gold": joyiswith.in/37. *Touch of Love* 1/5/17
Day 19: "Till Only Love Remains": joyiswith.in/38. *Touch of Peace* 4/18/19
Day 20: "Lift Up Your Eyes!": joyiswith.in/39. *Touch of Peace* 2/28/19
Day 21: "Sharing": joyiswith.in/40. *Touch of Peace* 5/31/19
Day 22: "Embrace Your Fears": joyiswith.in/41. *Touch of Peace* 3/13/20
Day 23: "When We Cooperate with Grace": joyiswith.in/42. *Touch of Peace* 8/9/19
Day 24: "Seeing the Possibilities": joyiswith.in/43. *Touch of Love* 3/16/17
Day 25: "Finding Calmness in the Midst of Activity": joyiswith.in/44. *Touch of Peace* 10/4/19
Day 26: "Weathering the Storm": joyiswith.in/45. *Touch of Peace* 2/14/20
Day 27: "Overcoming Conflict": joyiswith.in/46. *Touch of Peace* 11/1/19
Day 28: "Dissolving the Ego": joyiswith.in/47. *Touch of Peace* 2/7/20
Day 29: "Trusting First Impressions": joyiswith.in/48. *Touch of Light* 2/6/14
Day 30: "Do What You Can": joyiswith.in/49. *Touch of Peace* 9/20/19
Day 31: "Go On Alone!": joyiswith.in/50

The Paintings: To see more of Jyotish's paintings, visit jyotishart.com.

“You must stand unshaken amidst the crash of breaking worlds!”

It was **Paramhansa Yogananda,** the great modern mystic and author of *Autobiography of a Yogi,* who issued this soul-stirring exhortation.

How do we follow his great example and become warriors for the Light? *Stand Unshaken!* offers inspiration and practical guidance on how to live courageously during these turbulent times. Each secret of living fearlessly (one for each day of the month) is paired with a beautiful painting by Nayaswami Jyotish. This creates an environment in which you can absorb each message in a more receptive and uplifted state of consciousness.

Awaken within you the power to live in joy whatever your outward circumstances, and to bring that joy to others. Stand unshaken and you will be a light unto the world.

Nayaswamis Jyotish and Devi are dynamic emissaries of Paramhansa Yogananda, and global peace ambassadors. As Spiritual Directors of Ananda, and living examples of spiritual values in action, Jyotish and Devi travel the world, blessing people everywhere as they share Yogananda’s teachings and the practical and heart-opening path of Kriya Yoga that he brought. Swami Kriyananda, a direct disciple of Yogananda and Ananda’s founder, designated Jyotish as his spiritual successor.

Crystal Clarity Publishers
www.crystalclarity.com
800.424.1055